Prepare Him Room

ADVENT FOR BUSY CHRISTIANS

Prepare Him Room

ADVENT FOR BUSY CHRISTIANS

MARY LATELA

Liguori
ONE LIGUORI DRIVE
LIGUORI MO 63057-9999

© 1999, Liguori Publications
ISBN 0-7648-0397-2
Library of Congress Card
Number: 98-75662
Printed in the united States of America
99 00 01 02 03   5 4 3 2 1

"The King of Glory" © 1966, 1982, Willard
F. Jabusch. Administered by OCP Publications, 5536 N.E. Hassalo, Portland, OR
97213. All rights reserved. Used with permission.

Scripture quotations from the *New Revised
Standard Version of the Bible,* © 1989 by the
Division of Christian Education of the
National Council of the Churches of Christ
in the USA. Used with permission. All rights
reserved.

Cover design by Christine Kraus

Contents

Introduction

very year, Christians are reminded of the Incarnation of Jesus, the Son of God. Yet, at this very season—Advent, Christmas, and beyond—the world is so busy that making time for reflection may seem like just another of the many obligations of the season.

This collection of fourteen reflections, based on the birth narratives in Scripture and applied to contemporary life, empowers a busy Christian to refocus on the meaning of the season. These gentle meditations are aimed at recalling and reconnecting with Jesus through the Christmas story. The time commitment is minimal—just fourteen periods of quiet, fit into the season of giving. Give yourself this time and space to be with the One who comes, the One who journeys with you through life, and the One who will someday lead you home to the heart of the Creator God.

What Are We Awaiting?

hristmas comes early in the commercial world. The Halloween goodies are barely gone from the shelves of the department stores and supermarkets before the Christmas ornaments, wreaths, toys, and holiday foods appear. By the time Advent comes along, we may be tired of Christmas—unless we focus on trying to answer the question, "What are we waiting for?"

A friend learned quite a lesson some years back at Christmastide. Newly widowed, she threw herself into preparations for Christmas. Though her job kept her busy, and the upkeep of the house now rested solely on her shoulders, she made up her mind that she would "do" Christmas the way she always had. She would do all the decorating, write out all the cards, select and personally wrap all the presents, cook a huge dinner for the extended family, and on and on.

She tried so hard to make Christmas her way. Then on Christmas Eve, my friend came down with a bad case of the flu. She spent Christmas day in bed. And for the first time in the busy holiday season, she had some peace and quiet. In those quiet hours, she realized that Christmas is not about rushing around, not about doing and doing and doing until you get completely exhausted.

From her couch, my friend looked over at the creche with the delicately formed statues of Mary and Joseph and the baby Jesus, and she began to weep. Right there before her was the reason for Christmas, and she had almost missed it.

You've heard the saying, "Jesus is the reason for the season!" Whatever helps us to focus on that reality is good for us. Whatever distracts us from that reality cannot be good for us.

Jesus has already come. During this season, we read that he indeed was born of Mary, fulfilling the prophecies of old. Does Jesus Christ come again every time we celebrate Christmas? Is Jesus Christ born again? It depends on how you look at it.

A Christian is one who follows Jesus, who walks with Jesus, not because of a personal decision or because of an emotional need—or to be forgiven or to be included or to be loved—but because of a "call from above." During Advent, this period when you wait—in prayer and in silence and in reflection—for that wondrous Christmas feast, focus on rebirth. Ask Jesus Christ to be reborn in you—spiritually, powerfully. Ask Jesus—who came to us as a human person in order to understand you, and in order that you might understand him—to come again! Ask Jesus Christ to light the fire of love that he once offered to us, as infants or as adults, from whatever faith perspective we come. As you light candles around the Advent wreath to demonstrate the need for God's light to shine upon us as Christians, ask Jesus Christ to light a fire in your heart.

What are we waiting for? For Jesus Christ to reawaken us, to revive our love. Let us prepare to welcome him anew.

O come, O come, Emmanuel,
And ransom captive Israel.
That mourns in lonely exile here
Until the Son of God appears.
Rejoice! Rejoice!
Emmanuel shall come to thee, O Israel.

O COME, O COME, EMMANUEL

Making Room For Jesus

JEREMIAH 31:31-34
AND LUKE 1:13-17

he best way to send an idea," said scientist Robert Oppenheimer, "is to wrap it up in a person." Jesus was the incarnation of God. Jesus was the way that God sent this "idea" to humanity; there was and is no better way! Ignatius, one of the early Church fathers, explained that "by the Incarnation, God broke His silence." Less scholarly an explanation, but equally to the point, is the remark of a little girl who said, "Some people couldn't hear God's inside whisper and so God sent Jesus to tell them out loud."

The Gospel of John declares dramatically, "The Word became flesh and lived among us" (1:14). The Word, that living expression of God, is our connection with God's truth and power and glory. The Word brings each of us into the heart of Creation. We are invited into the personal presence of the lover of our souls. What a great and wonderful blessing!

Remember Jeremiah, the prophet called to bring a message of doom to the people of Israel? Imagine his astonishment when he hears the latest from the Lord. Now, God is making new rules. Now, God will no longer make obedience the test of whether the people are living right. Now, God is going straight for the heart. "The days are surely coming, says the Lord, when I will make a new covenant with the house of Israel and the house of Judah...this is the covenant that I will make with the house of Israel after those days, says the Lord: I will put my law within them, and I will write it on their hearts; and I will be their God, and they shall be my people."

This is wonderful news...as long as people make room in their hearts for God!

Our lives are cluttered with an amazing array of responsibilities and time-consuming activities. During the period before Christmas, we may feel particularly overwhelmed with everything we have to do. As we look around and see our homes and our sanctuary filled with wonderful things, beautiful things, let us remember to MAKE ROOM FOR JESUS.

We put in place the greenery, the creche, and the candles. Yet, these symbols and signs are meant to remind us of the Christmas journey, not clutter our way. And the only way to be sure that we are not taken over by the material things of this season is to keep watch over our hearts. We are in a period of waiting. The creche is empty. The star has not lit the way, though streets and homes are brightly lit. The angels have not announced the good tidings—not yet!

But as we recall and relive the Christmas story, we are involved in a more immediate story, reconnecting with Jesus in a more powerful way, strengthening the ties that are there, and deepening our sense of what Jesus Christ has done and continues to do in our lives.

First, we can try to make time for Jesus: "Whisper a prayer in the morning, whisper a prayer at night." We can make our priorities clear, and place time with the Lord at the top of our list of things to do, knowing that even a few moments here and there will help. We can pray together with our faith community, and listen to the Scriptures, the music, and the silence.

Second, we can open our hearts to emotional healing. For many of us, this season is bittersweet. We may be far from our families, or we may be mourning the death of a loved one and feel that loss most acutely at this season. We may be dealing with unpleasant memories of Christmases past. We may be depressed or lonely or anxious. Now, we may not experience a miracle that will free us from all that, but we can be open to a little bit of healing, a little bit of comfort, from the only one who really understands what we are going through.

Third, we can open our hearts to spiritual healing. Most of us have doubts about our faith from time to time, and the Christmas season is no exception. We may feel that our relationship with God is too sporadic to count on now. We may come to church out of a sense of duty or habit, but Friends, God will take us as we are, and work in us as long as we are open to this spiritual healing.

And will life be different? ABSOLUTELY! Think about Zechariah, minding his own business—serious, sacred business, of course—but what a night! He and his wife Elizabeth would have a son, a very special person who would prepare the way for the one whom they were awaiting.

The angel said to him, "Do not be afraid,

Zechariah, for your prayer has been heard. Your wife Elizabeth will bear you a son, and you will name him John. You will have joy and gladness, and many will rejoice at his birth, for he will be great in the sight of the Lord...He will turn many of the people of Israel to the Lord their God...to make ready a people prepared for the Lord."

God enters the life of ordinary people, and things turn upside down. When Zechariah went home to Elizabeth, he could not speak for a long period of time. We sense that his heart was opened instead, and that there was room for the Lord to work in him.

When Christmas morning comes, it's not over! If we "do Advent well"—if we lead with our hearts, if we open our hearts and make room for Jesus, not just on the surface, but within—life will be really different.

The Lord put the idea of promise into the hearts of Zechariah and Elizabeth. The Lord put the idea of incredible love into the heart of Mary of Nazareth. The Lord puts the idea of hope and fellowship and commitment and giftedness into our hearts—here and now.

Howard Thurmond writes: "When the song of the angels is silent, When the star in the sky is gone; When the kings and princes are home; When the shepherds are again tending their sheep; When the manger is darkened and still—The work of Christmas begins: To find the lost; to heal the broken; to feed the hungry; To rebuild the nations; To bring peace among people; To befriend the lonely; To release the prisoner; To make music in the heart."[1]

How silently, how silently
the wondrous gift is given
So God imparts to human hearts
the blessing of His heaven.
We hear the Christmas angels,
the great glad tidings tell;
O come with us, abide with us,
Our Lord Immanuel.

O LITTLE TOWN OF BETHLEHEM

Do You Believe in Angels?

LUKE 1:17-79

o you believe in angels? Of course you do! Remember the angel who wrestled with Jacob all night long, preparing him to lead his people? Remember the angel who came to Zechariah to tell him about the grand mission of his son, John the Baptizer? Remember Gabriel, who came and told Mary the good news that she was to be the mother of Jesus?

We have to admit that the Bible accepts the existence of angels without question. Actually, Jewish tradition is filled with references to angels. In our time, we are asked once again, "Do you believe in angels?" And I think the implication is a bit different. What people are asking is, "Do you believe that angels are working in your life now, that they serve as messengers of God in the here and now, that they guard you from harm these days?" This is more complicated, because it is subjective. It means that in order to answer, I have to look inside myself, into the secret places, and wonder about how God moves in my life.

If I have forgotten about my guardian angel, does my forgetting send her away? I don't recall an interaction with an angel, yet does my lack of recognition negate the possibility? Hmmm.

I met a young mother who talked about the death of her young daughter in a bicycle accident. This woman was in such pain that she could not function. One day, to get away from the house and the reminders of her loss, she walked aimlessly down the road. She was so distraught that she fell to the ground, weeping. An elderly woman hugged her and held her while she cried. After a while, the tears stopped and the mother got up to go home. When she turned to thank the old woman, she was gone. And she never saw her again. The mother believes that God sent an angel to her on that day. No one can convince her otherwise. Some may say she was dreaming, that grief clouded her judgment, and yet, who can really say?

As we read in Luke's gospel, Zechariah, a priest of Israel, entered the Holy of Holies of the Temple, to pray to Yahweh. Zechariah encountered an angel. We don't know how this happened, and the only source would be Zechariah himself, but he was sure that an angel came, and who are we to argue? The incredible news—that a son, a very special son, would be born to Zechariah and his wife Elizabeth, HAD TO BE news from God.

That son was destined to go ahead of Jesus, to prepare the way for Jesus. That son was to be called John, who came to be known as the Baptist, because he called people to repent of their sins and baptized them in the River Jordan.

In Greek, the word *angelos* means "messenger." An angel is a celestial being serving as a messenger or intermediary between God and humankind. In ancient Greek religion, in Judaism and Christianity, and in Islam, angels are divine messengers sent to us to instruct, inform, or command. An angel can also act as a guardian, or heavenly warrior, or cosmic power. In traditional Israelite thought, angels were assumed to have the form of human males, and so they were sometimes mistaken for men.

Seraphim, cherubim, thrones, dominations, virtues, powers, principalities, archangels, and angels—these are the nine choirs of angels. Each has a different task. According to the Bible, cherubim were placed at the east side of the Garden of Eden to prevent human beings from reentering. In Ezekiel, we read fantastic, detailed descriptions of cherubim. Of the archangels, we are most familiar with Michael, Gabriel, Raphael, and Uriel. Michael, according to the Book of Daniel, is presumed to be the leader of the angels and guardian angel of Israel. It is in the Book of Enoch, which is not part of the canon, that we hear the story of the battle between Michael and Lucifer, the faithful versus the rebellious angels. Uriel is considered the namesake of Jerusalem. Gabriel is the heavenly messenger who appears in order to reveal God's will. In the New Testament, he comes to Zechariah to announce the coming birth of John the Baptist. Gabriel also visits Mary, who is to be the mother of Jesus.

After his son John was born, Zechariah prayed like a man struck by the Holy Spirit, like the prophets speaking, profound and inspired. And this makes sense—God touches a life and that life is forever changed, that soul sings a new song, a song of salvation and deliverance and joy and hope. Did you ever feel inspired? What was that like? If you are tempted to dismiss this inquiry without a second thought, WAIT!

When have you felt God has touched you? When you hear the children singing in church, do you brush away a tear? Why? Somehow, a simple act by our children can move us, awaken us to something we may have forgotten—our need to feel something sacred in our ordinary lives.

As we prepare our hearts for Christmas, for the coming again of Jesus into our lives, we yearn to recognize again the sacred in our lives. And God is sacred, and anything that God sends has a sacred quality.

Many of us enjoy watching the television show, "Touched by an Angel." This program is about the quiet way these "messengers from God" help people turn their lives around, not by bold intervention, but simply by their presence. One particular episode was a bit different from the rest. It was about what happens when we die. A man came close to death and had a frightful experience of what lay ahead—he saw "the light," yet felt he was about to be swallowed by darkness. Even the angel of death was somber. It was powerful to see so dramatically that yes, God is love, and yes, God plans for us to return home to heaven after our brief stay on earth. But we have a choice. And if we choose to keep God out of our lives here, how can we expect to know God when we die? In the show, the angel of death asks the sinful man, "Don't you want to look into a face that you recognize?" Of course, we do. And we will recognize God's face IF AND ONLY IF we have practiced looking for God's face in this phase of our eternal lives.

The time before Christmas can be beautiful, but it can also be hectic, frustrating, and tiring. We need to guard against getting too wrapped up in our own plans for holiday preparation, rushing here and there, knowing that we are growing more and more tense, but still rushing to get everything done that WE WANT. Perhaps we need to be cautious about our expectations for Christmas. We do not always have a "merry little Christmas." We do not always "hear the angels sing," and we do not always experience "peace on earth, good will toward all." Our Christmas is real-life, sometimes complicated, sometimes lonely, sometimes sad and empty, too noisy and too bright, with too many people showing up, too many difficult relationships to maintain, too many inconvenient delays, not enough of "silent night" or "holy night."

If we forget who and what we are waiting for, we may substitute our own plans for God's plans, which makes it difficult to be open to what God wants us to see this year. Friends, we need more of Bethlehem for Christmas! We need to remember that night when Mary and Joseph were so far away from home, when Mary was frightened about giving birth because she was young and because her mother was not there with her. We need to see Joseph, struggling with his angels and his dreams to figure out how to handle it all. We need to think of the shepherds—tired from their hard work, forgotten by the world as they toiled in complete darkness, torn between their terror at a mysterious light and their need to take care of their sheep. We need to think of Jesus, coming in the night, into the arms of his mother, into the protection of his father, into a world full of promise and yet so fickle.

Have you ever heard the expression, "Be careful

when you welcome the stranger, because you may be welcoming an angel unaware"? I say, when you welcome Jesus, expect anything! Expect everything! You will see the stranger in a new light. You will see your friends in a new light. You will see your life more clearly and with fewer illusions. You will know Jesus as he was in Bethlehem, as he was in Jerusalem, as he is today, in our midst, if only you take the time and make the effort to pay attention.

May God help you to focus on the message and on the messenger during this holy season.

Angels we have heard on high,
Sweetly singing o'er the plains.
And the mountains in reply
Echo back their joyous strains.
Gloria in excelsis Deo! Gloria in excelsis Deo!

ANGELS WE HAVE HEARD ON HIGH

Mary, the Mother of Jesus

LUKE 1:26-38

Denise Levertov describes the Annunciation in *Breathing the Water:*
"This was the minute no one speaks of, when she could still refuse. A breath unbreathed, Spirit, suspended, waiting. She did not cry, 'I cannot, I am not worthy,' nor, 'I have not the strength.' She did not submit with gritted teeth, raging, coerced. Bravest of all humans, consent illumined her. The room filled with its light, the lily glowed in it, and the iridescent wings. Consent, courage unparalleled, opened her utterly."[2]

The Scriptures tell us very little about Mary. Some say this has to do with the male authorship of the Bible. Some say this lack of information is related to the subordinate role of women in ancient Israel. Others believe that Mary cannot be prominent because that would take away from our focus on Jesus.

Mary is surrounded by mystery. She is a figure about whom we know very little, and about whom we can speculate almost without boundaries. Mary of Nazareth. Mary, barely beyond childhood herself, is called by God to bear a child of her own. Mary is asked to perform the intimate task of carrying a child within her, and this child is Jesus. Does Mary's response to Gabriel's invitation show that she is a model of passivity? No. If we listen closely, we can hear the voice of a strong woman, a woman who questioned Gabriel, a woman whom Gabriel did not leave until she had spoken her own words of acceptance.

What do we need to believe about Mary? I think we need to remember that Mary was a woman, that Mary was a mother, that Mary loved Jesus more than we could measure. As a faith community, we need to remember that Mary was the mother of Jesus, our Redeemer. She was the vessel, if you will, for bringing Jesus into the world, and Mary somehow lives on because of her role in the life of Jesus and the life of the Church.

What we cannot say is that Mary was somehow divine, or that she was superhuman, or an angel herself. We can learn something about the way God entered into Mary, and the way God used Mary. We can realize something profound about our capacity to be instruments of God for good: the good of our own family and friends, the good of those we don't know, the good of the communion of saints. For Mary was a simple, poor young woman when the Holy Spirit filled her. That presence changed her dramatically, but it did not transform her into something other than a good human person called upon to live a life that was extraordinary for its commitment to doing God's will ALWAYS! "Thy will be done."

Jesus taught us to pray to his Father using these words, "Thy will be done." In the gospel narrative, Mary responds to the invitation to be the mother of Jesus with the words, "Thy will be done." We may hear her words as the inevitable response to a demanding God, but that seems incomplete. It seems more accurate to understand Mary as one who willed that her life be completely in tune with the will of God, that the symphony of her existence on earth be the melody of God's song singing in her and through her.

Not yet married, Mary was called to be a mother. She could not have known the full implications of Jesus' life when she said "Yes" to becoming his mother. We see throughout the Scripture that she came to understand her son's life gradually, even as Jesus came to understand himself. The surprise for Mary was the untimely message about Jesus' coming birth. Now we know how it all turned out— that Joseph was faithful to her, that she was not punished by death according to the law, that they went ahead with their lives. Thus, we may not have sufficient awe of Mary's courage. She must have been deeply troubled by the news of this pregnancy.

But, Mary somehow mustered the courage that she never imagined she would need. She did so with God's help, yes, but very concretely with the help of Joseph, her betrothed husband, and her family. Mary went to visit her older cousin, Elizabeth, and received encouragement from her.

And isn't that how we manage to get through what seem to be incredible situations? Not alone, surely. We need the support of other people as we try to discern and follow the will of God. Mary's response to Gabriel's request and her response to God's will throughout the life of Jesus raise challenges for us. We are challenged to compare our own responses to what God asks of us to Mary's "fiat."

What unusual challenges have you faced in your life? How did you respond? As you make difficult decisions, what are your thoughts and feelings? When has someone asked you to do something that seemed impossible, beyond your capabilities, or something that might alienate others? Where do you draw the line when it comes to your response to God?

In the gospels, Mary sings a song of joy. This might be our theme song. "My soul trembles in the presence of the loving Creator and my spirit prepares itself to walk hand in hand with the God who saved Israel because I have been accepted by God as a simple helpmate. Yes, forever in the life of humankind people will sing of this loving encounter: through remembering this moment, the faithful will know all things are possible and holy is the place within me where God lives. God's tender fingers reach out from age to age to touch the softened inner spaces of those who open their souls in hope. I have experienced the creative power of God's embracing arms and I know the cleansing fire of unconditional love. I am freed from all earthly authority and know my bonding to the Author of all earthly things."[3]

God calls us to give birth to the holy in our lives. God invites you and me to be God-bearers, to reveal God's love and grace, to embody God in the world. In some sense, we are invited to continue the Incarnation by living out the continual coming of God in Christ. God invites us, and, like Mary, we choose. The call to bear Christ in us is definitely not a call to passivity or conformity. It is a call to radical assent to whatever God wills, to wherever God takes us, to whatever we encounter in this life. As you wait, as you prepare to renew your connection to Jesus at Christmastide, remember that he waits to hear us say, "Yes, Lord, come."

What child is this, who, laid to rest,
On Mary's lap is sleeping?
Whom angels greet with anthems sweet,
While shepherds watch are keeping?
This, this is Christ the King,
Whom shepherds guard and angels sing;
Haste, haste, to bring Him laud,
The babe, the son of Mary.

WHAT CHILD IS THIS

Angels, Angels, Everywhere!

ISAIAH 12:1-6 AND
MATTHEW 1:18-25

wonder what Joseph was thinking when Mary told him she was to have a child. Did he believe her about that encounter with the angel, that stuff about the Holy Spirit? I wonder if he was angry or afraid; I wonder if he told anyone.

The Scripture reads: "Joseph, being a righteous man and unwilling to expose her to public disgrace, planned to dismiss her quietly." This sounds very harsh; were there no other options? Before he could do anything, however, he encountered an angel who somehow calmed his fears and made everything all right.

The angel said to him in a dream: "Joseph, son of David, do not be afraid to take Mary as your wife, for the child conceived in her is from the Holy Spirit." This narrative assumes that Mary and Joseph had all the answers ahead of time: that they never wondered why their marriage started in such an "irregular" way, that they never wondered why God acted in their lives this way. I think that Joseph WAS afraid. I think that Mary WAS afraid. But something kept them together, kept them going, kept them waiting for their child, not knowing quite whom to expect, not understanding all of this very clearly. And what could explain Joseph's sudden reversal from wanting to reject Mary to wanting to marry her? It must have been something spectacular. It must have been an angel calling to him in a loud voice, or perhaps a still, small voice that Joseph perceived to be a message from God.

In Matthew's gospel, Joseph is helped out of a number of tricky situations by an angel. And the story resonates with us because we know that sometimes, when there seems to be no place to go, when we seem to be in terribly dire straits, a solution comes, seemingly out of nowhere.

In the midst of Advent we can rejoice. We can give thanks that God reaches out to us through the Christmas story in ways that are sometimes incredible. As Paul writes in the Letter to the Church at Philippi: "Rejoice in the Lord always; again I will say, Rejoice. Let your gentleness be known to everyone. The Lord is near" (Philippians 4:4-5).

In her book, *Where Angels Walk*, Joan Wester Anderson writes: "Do you believe in angels? I always did, at least in theory. After all, angels are mentioned over 300 times in Scripture; they seem to be busy and involved in the lives of everyone from Tobit to the Blessed Virgin. But truly meaningful creatures? In this day and age? As a journalist, I was especially skeptical."[4]

Then Mrs. Anderson tells of a remarkable event. On a December night in 1983, her son Tim and his roommate were driving home from college to spend Christmas with the family. Their journey was complicated by record-low temperatures, minus 30 degrees by 1 a.m., when they got to Indiana. There, the car stalled, miles from anywhere, on a road bordered by cornfields. There were no lights in the distance, no place to go to for help.

As this was happening, Mrs. Anderson was at home praying for Tim, worrying about his delayed arrival. "God, please send someone to help him." As Tim told the story later, the boys suddenly saw the headlights of a tow truck blazing behind them, although they hadn't seen it approach. The driver took them to a place of safety. But when they turned around to pay him, he had vanished. And there were no truck tracks in the snow.

Anderson says, "I pondered this happening for a long time. Could the 'someone' God sent have been an angel, maybe even Tim's guardian angel? Did heaven intercede today? I decided to find out." And so, over the next few years, when giving a speech, teaching a class, or just talking with friends, she would share Tim's miracle. Other people began to share similar stories. And she saw that people are very much aware that God is with us, and that God truly cares.

A stranger often appears at just the right time, just when someone needs help, and then is seen no more. An angel? Why not? And often, God sends a spouse or special friend to bring us this reassurance. There are human angels, too. People come to help us, and perhaps we too encounter someone at just the right moment to dramatically change their life. Remember this reflection:

"You never know when someone may catch a dream from you. You never know when a little word, or something you may do, may open up the windows of a mind that seeks the light. The way you live may not matter at all, but you never know—it might. And just in case it could be that another's life, through you, might possibly change for the better with a broader and brighter view. It seems it might be worth a try at pointing the way to the right. Of course, it may not matter at all, but then again—it might." (Author unknown)

I think we are apt to be a little overwhelmed by the busyness of this holy season, by the distractions of the commercial world, and perhaps from our own need to DO MORE than we really CAN, or to BE MORE than we really ARE. Let's remember that we are not alone, and that God's help is all around. But we do need to pay attention!

Let's take some time each day to consider God's infinite kindness as it enters our own lives, particularly at surprising times, when we feel alone or particularly stressed. Now, recall a time when a kindness was done to you—unexpectedly. A time when you felt valued, perhaps even loved. Think of the person who granted you this kindness and made you feel whole and worthwhile. Breathe a silent "thank you."

Think of the grandmothers and grandfathers who cared for your parents. Think of your parents when they most loved you, whether you were aware of it or not. Think of the one who nursed you, bathed you, and cared for you when you were an infant. Imagine who did that for them when they were tiny. Imagine in front of you all the kind women and men you know or have heard about. Think of those who serve others. Imagine the women and men who gave their lives over the centuries to protect the ones they loved. See in your mind those who brought healing through the centuries and millennia, who were instruments of miraculous things. Hold this love in your heart! Share this kindness and compassion with the world.

Recall—whenever you want to—God's power to reach out to you when you need it the most. Remember this as you wait for Christmas!

I wonder as I wander out under the sky,
How Jesus the Savior did come for to die
For poor ord'nar' people like you and like I;
I wonder as I wander out under the sky.

I WONDER AS I WANDER

The Longest Night

ISAIAH 42:1-11 AND
JOHN 1:1-14

uring Advent, on December 21, we encounter the shortest day of the year, and that night is the longest night. What does that mean for you as you consider the Christmas story and how it impacts your life now?

The birth story is not simply about birth. We who are blessed with faith in Jesus know that this very life, with its sometimes short days and very long nights, is somehow similar to that great birth, awakening, enlightenment, resurrection, into the heart of God forever.

"In the beginning was the Word, and the Word was with God, and the Word was God. He was in the beginning with God. All things came into being through him, and without him not one thing came into being. What has come into being in him was life, and the life was the light of all people. The light shines in the darkness, and the darkness did not overcome it."

So begins the Gospel of John, a very mysterious beginning, all about the WORD, the Logos, and what happened before the beginning of time. Jesus with God in the beginning, and Jesus with us on earth. The light shining in the darkness—light so bright that we can't even imagine it; light so warm that we can't understand it; light so permanent that we will never know darkness again.

Some nights pass quickly, and others seem to last forever. Do you remember the song, "Help Me Make It Through the Night"? Surely, you have known those nights, when your child was sick, or when you waited for someone to come home, or when you were tired and lonely and you couldn't sleep. Somehow, even from the beginning, God has understood about the longest night, our waiting for the dawn that will truly bring daylight to our lives.

In Isaiah we read what is called the First Servant Song. "Here is my servant, whom I uphold, my chosen, in whom my soul delights; I have put my spirit upon him; he will bring forth justice to the nations." Who is speaking? It is God! God speaks to the people!

God speaks to the servant. WHO IS THIS SERVANT? The servant is called to bring justice to the nations, to be silent and very caring, yet to concentrate his efforts tirelessly on justice. The servant is to have an impact even on the distant future. This task, then, is enormous: establishing justice, seemingly for the whole world. The prophet has international events in mind, both present and future. Who has the power to bring justice to the nations? Who has the power to bring justice tempered with compassion? Well, only God.

This passage reminds us that God is the creator, and God can do all things. God created everything: the heavens and the earth and all that fills them. God created the human beings that live on the earth and who receive their very breath from God.

Who is this servant? He is to be a king! Only a king has the awesome task of assuring and ensuring justice in his kingdom. The Israelite king was charged with maintaining justice.

Who is this servant? He is to be a prophet. Persons like Elijah and Elisha became prophets when the Spirit of the Lord came upon them. The gift of the Spirit empowers the servant, too. This servant will not break those who are already bruised, or quench the flame of even the faintest light.

The servant, then, is identified with those he is sent to aid.

The servant is to be a shining light to the nation, to the peoples, and to the world.

The original identity of the Suffering Servant described in these verses from Isaiah is unknown. Was he the unnamed prophet whose words we now read? Did the prophet describe someone the community knew so well that he did not need to name him? Was this a vision of one who was to come, or someone who had lived as an exile among exiles? We do not know. What we have done with this description is use it to identify the servant/leader of any time and place whose image matches this stark outline.

And most importantly, we identify this servant with Jesus, who came to live among us. "I have taken you by the hand and kept you; I have given you as a covenant to the people, a light to the nations, to open the eyes that are blind, to bring out the prisoners from the dungeon, from the prison those who sit in darkness. I am the LORD, that is my name."

Jesus is this Servant-King! We are called into this life, and sometimes we wonder if this is all there is. And sometimes we wonder if it could get any better. And sometimes we are able to say, "I believe in LIFE! I believe in the Creator! I believe in Eternity!"

There is a story about an eight-year-old girl who said that she heard angels singing. Her parents were concerned, and they consulted a therapist. This wise person told them, "This child has simply not forgotten. Little babies can hear the angels singing—how else do you explain their little smiles and knowing looks? But as they grow up, and are trained to live in a no-nonsense world, they forget." This special child had held on to her birth gift a little longer than most. Why do we forget? Perhaps this is the time for us to remember those singing angels.

We hear the word *generosity* frequently during this season. Often it is associated with a request for money: "Your generosity would be appreciated." When we learn the origin of the word, many of the associations are related to Christmas. Yet none of them have to do with obligation, commerce, acquisitiveness, or pressure to perform, which often characterize modern seasonal giving. Instead, the root of *generosity* seems to come from something simple but great, something fertile, something being born.

Through the ages, winter has been a time to celebrate a rebirth of the earth, a renewal of the creation upon which our very lives depend. The Earth Mother was honored for her generosity. Giving and sharing in a time of hardship was an act of faith in future abundance. In the Christian tradition, the wise men from the East brought gifts to honor the divine child. Later, Saint Nicholas, or Kris Kringle, extended this generosity to children of the poor. As he extended his love to children, he honored the divine child in them. At this time, express your generosity as an act of faith in the source of your abundance.

"And the Word became flesh and lived among us, and we have seen his glory, the glory as of a father's only son, full of grace and truth."

Let us give to others in honor of the divine child who came into this world a long time ago and still dwells in each of us, in our hearts.

Let us open our hearts. There is love enough to share, love enough to make it through the night of this life, with its joys, and shadows, and confusion, love enough to make it into that great dawn.

They looked up and saw a star
Shining in the east, beyond them far,
And to the earth it gave great light,
And so it continued both day and night.
Noel, Noel, Noel, Noel,
Born is the King of Israel.

THE FIRST NOEL

A Child Shall Lead Them

ISAIAH 11:1-10 AND
LUKE 1:66-80

e are often amused by the insights of a child. We are struck by the honesty and candor, by the simple and straightforward responses to profound questions. And yet, do we want that child to be our leader, the one who makes the decisions about our future? Someday, maybe, but not yet.

I wonder how the people of Israel felt about the words of Isaiah the prophet:

"The wolf shall live with the lamb, the leopard shall lie down with the kid, the calf and the lion and the fatling together, and a little child shall lead them. The cow and the bear shall graze, their young shall lie down together; and the lion shall eat straw like the ox."

A Child Shall Lead Them

What must this have sounded like to the people of Israel, who were at the edge of extinction, their kingdom collapsing and their future a long exile in a faraway land? *A child shall lead them?* Impossible. And what kind of kingdom would place together the lion and the calf—the wild and the domesticated alike—the enemy and the friend? What kind of peaceable kingdom would this be? It couldn't be. And yet Isaiah's words seem to foretell the coming of a child who will be the king, namely Jesus. It reflects as well the coming of another child, John the Baptist, who would prepare the way for this peaceable kingdom.

A Child Shall Lead Them

But how do we react to a child who is different, who marches to a different drummer, who seems too wise for us, who seems to have insights that are striking? And in general, how do we react to anyone who is different, someone like John the Baptist, someone like you and me, at times? For a child who is destined for great things, like John the Baptist, what were the expectations?

The song of Zechariah is pretty powerful: "You, child, will be called the prophet of the Most High; for you will go before the Lord to prepare his ways, to give knowledge of salvation to his people by the forgiveness of their sins."

How hard is it to grow up sensing that more is expected of you, even if you are not told what those expectations are?

We read nothing in the Bible about John's childhood, nor about what we would call his adolescence. Some of us may have felt during our own adolescence that we were different from everyone else, that our problems were much greater than everybody else's, that by some mistake we were left with our family, when we really should have grown up in another, different family. And our sense that we might be called to NOT simply follow in the footsteps of our parents, or NOT do what everyone else was doing, was hard to take. Who wants to stand out, unless it's in the acceptable ways—on the football field, or in the advanced math class, or in the church choir?

And what about John the Baptist? We understand that John was called to follow a different path than his friends and relatives. How must that have felt? He was called to a very different life, different even from the call of his cousin, Jesus.

What did his neighbors think? Did they offer support, or did they try not to talk about him, for the sake of his elderly parents, Elizabeth and Zechariah? "The child grew and became strong in spirit, and he was in the wilderness until the day he appeared publicly to Israel." He lived as a hermit, as a man of God in the wilderness, and was probably considered very eccentric. The center of his mission was to make way the path for Jesus. He was a blunt man who condemned the unrepentant sinners. But he was also a man of peace, a preacher of nonviolence in a very violent world.

In Luke, we read of the mission of John: "By the tender mercy of our God, the dawn from on high will break upon us, to give light to those who sit in darkness and in the shadow of death, to guide our feet into the way of peace."

John the Baptist, the young man, brought mercy and understanding to the people who were caught up in their own little worlds. I wonder how much attention we pay to those who come in peace, who do not consider violence a solution to their problems. Are we are ready to accept their counter-cultural vision?

A Child Shall Lead Them

We have become very accustomed to violence in our society. Innocent people are hurt and killed every day. This kind of news grabs our attention for a brief moment; we lament the prevalence of violence, and wonder how we can be safe. Then we try to move on.

In this world where evil seems to be so common, we need to think about gaining the power to transform evil by peaceable ways. According to Mohandes Gandhi, "Violence does not ever overcome evil; it suppresses it for the time being to rise later with redoubled vigor. Nonviolence, on the other hand, puts an end to evil, for it converts the evildoer." Friend, we always have the power to pray, and prayer works, because our compassion for other children of God is powerful and because God is powerful.

I need to believe that a child will lead us. I wonder if we are praying enough for all the children and for those who care for them. God hears all our honest prayers, without conditions. Friend, we are not powerless to change the world, if we are willing to open our own heart, just a little. We CAN pray. And we MUST pray. This is one way that we can face the evil of our time and impact it. And we who are called Christians are definitely connected to the root of Jesse. We are all called, in our own way—perhaps not in a public, dramatic way—to be like John, to be like those who serve God with righteousness and dignity, to serve all God's children, whatever the consequences.

As we continue to work through Advent, we might want to be sure that our own hearts are loving, that our motives are pure, that we are willing to live with the effects of the coming of Jesus into our lives.

Angels, from the realms of glory,
Wing your flight o'er all the earth;
Ye, who sang creation's story,
Now proclaim Messiah's birth:
Come and worship,
Come and worship,
Worship Christ, the new-born King.

ANGELS, FROM THE REALMS OF GLORY

Who Is This King of Glory?

**ISAIAH 61:1-3 AND
MATTHEW 1:18-25**

*The king of glory comes, the nation rejoices
Open the gates before him, lift up your
voices.*

or those who met Jesus about 2000 years
ago, this was the question: "Who are you?"
And his response was in the form of a question: "Who do you say that I am?" The
coming of Jesus is a drama, a real-life drama
full of irony. We need only consider the circumstances
of his birth to see that the life of Jesus was full of
seeming contradictions. We are filled with questions
about Jesus and yet, in the very mystery of him, we
have all the answers we could possibly need.

Jesus presented God's offer of salvation through
his life, his death, and his teaching, particularly his
teaching on the commandments of love—loving
God and loving our neighbor as ourselves.

The love that Jesus taught us has to do with
complete submission to God's will, with forgetting
self, not because we are worthless, but because our
worth comes from God, and all the good that we
do belongs to God. The love that Jesus taught us

has to do with discovering who we are and from whom we come, and living accordingly.

Who is the king of glory? How shall we call him? He is Emmanuel, the promised of ages.

Emmanuel means "God with us." Now, how much of this do you think Mary understood? How much of this did Joseph understand? How much of this did the shepherds who followed the star and the wise men who journeyed from afar understand? We don't know for sure. We can be fairly certain that no one fully understood Jesus, and that getting to know him more and more was an adventure and a challenge.

Have you ever met someone who truly touched your life? How did you understand the impact they had on you and the meaning of your encounter? Most likely, this understanding did not come all at once. You probably came to know that person little by little, as you added up the clues and figured in your own responses, your own thoughts and feelings. When we love another human person, we may say it was "love at first sight," but we continue to grow in love as we get to know that person, and recognize how their presence in our life changes us. How is our life changed by the presence of Jesus, of "God-with-us"?

In all of Galilee, in city or village, he goes among his people curing their illness.

Jesus brought healing. But what was the illness he came to cure? Yes, some folks struggled with physical ailments, and when Jesus cured them, it was called "a miracle." And many people struggled with spiritual ailments, with discouragement, with despair, with exhaustion from suffering and from waiting so long to be redeemed. And they all struggled with sin, the only thing that can separate us from God. Jesus cured them by offering himself as the medicine, and as the radical surgery for sin. He suffered and died for us, so that we might live forever with God.

David's son, our savior and brother.

How can this be? Jesus was a descendant of David, but he was much more than that. His royalty came not from human lineage, but from all eternity. He is the Savior who died for us back then, but who also continues to save us from our sin by interacting with us one-on-one as our personal Lord and Savior. In other words, Jesus died for all humankind once, and that was enough. And Jesus continues to live—in our hearts, in our community of faith, in the world today, wherever people remember and follow him.

In some ways, our celebration of Christmas is a reminder, a bookmark in the calendar of our life. But a bookmark doesn't guarantee that we have read the book, that we have understood what we have read, or that we can been changed by our encounter. What I'm saying is that Christmas is a reminder, but we are free to browse, or to participate fully. And full participation in Christmas means that when our Advent is completed, we enter into the life of Jesus, not for just a day, or for a few weeks, but for always. We are called to make or renew our commitment. We need to read between the lines, we need to reflect on what we see, we need to ponder the word of Scripture and the life of Jesus as it impacts us today.

He conquered sin and death, he truly has risen. And he will share with us his heavenly vision.

You know, because Christmas is celebrated in the dead of winter, the days are short and the nights are very long. We may miss the sunshine and the warmth, and the gentle rain and the rainbows. But we do have the clear sky and the stars to remind us that the light of the world—Jesus Christ—can illumine our darkness and erase our shadows. In the silence of our hearts, in the midst of noise and music and laughter, we know very well that Christmas is only the beginning of a journey that will take us into eternity.

What is born in us now—love and compassion in the midst of ordinary days and nights—needs to grow. And God will help us to grow and bloom through our response to the promise of Christmas— the promise that this child who is born to us is the king of glory, and the king of glory is a king of gentleness and strength, of power and dependence, of childhood and long years, of a young mother and her baby, of the Lord God and God's only Son.

Sing then of David's Son, our savior and brother;
In all of Galilee was never another.
He conquered sin and death; he truly has risen,
And he will share with us his heavenly vision.
The King of Glory comes, the nation rejoices,
open the gates before him lift up your voices!

THE KING OF GLORY

Holy Night

LUKE 2:1-18

t is time. The weeks and months of waiting and wondering and planning quickly dissolve into birth and new life and promise! Suddenly the coming is upon us, and time is dissolved. There is only the present in its gleaming, stark clarity. No past or future, there is only now! We live in the moment—the promised one bursts forth! NEW LIFE SINGS OUT! The miracle of Christmas—the miracle of Jesus coming into the world—has arrived!

Something incredible seems to happen when folks go to church on a night like this. Emotionally, people come as they are. Some are lonely and they wonder what life is all about. They wonder why they are here, why they continue to struggle. Some come feeling rushed and frustrated, knowing there is so much left to do. But in this brief encounter, at least for this short time, they find meaning.

We all seek happiness, love, and direction. And we can see these more clearly tonight. All over the world, people gather at Christmas, whether in the Holy Land, or in Europe, or in the Northern Plains of the United States. People come to church because of unspoken needs, because in their hearts they believe—or want to believe—that Someone is waiting. People come to church to meet God and, at

Christmas, God's presence is palpable. The air is full of expectation, the silence is broken only by music, laughter and, often, gentle tears.

Most of us celebrate Christmas because we seek to be filled up with whatever we are missing—faith or hope or love. How do you sense Jesus coming into the world? Coming to you and me again? Do you envision the star? Do you hear the angels singing? Do you believe that you WILL find the child in the manger and his mother, Mary, and the shepherds and the wise men?

At Christmas, it's hard to say, "I am not worthy." Jesus Christ became a human being for you and for me, that's all. From the humble birth in a stable through the obscure childhood in Nazareth, into the turbulent times of public ministry, and through his death and unto his Resurrection, Jesus broke down all the barriers to eternity, all obstacles to our connection with the Almighty.

Jesus came into a world that was as imperfect as our own. He startled the world with his candor. He challenged the world with his message of love and forgiveness. He transformed human persons by his loving existence—by teaching them, and bringing them healing of body and spirit, by forgiving them and by showing them how to forgive.

Has your love for another person led you to journey to an unknown place? Did you come here to live when your family moved here, or when you were married? Then you understand what it means to start a whole new life in a new place. You understand the challenge of shifting gears, of adjusting. The book, *Nothing to Do but Stay*[5], is about pioneer folks who came to the Dakotas to make a brighter future, and who suffered terribly in order to reach their goals. They did stay, and they wanted to stay. The strength they developed, and the courage they mustered made it possible to do what they had never imagined they could do.

Christmas Mass is a kind of rest stop along our journey through life with Jesus. We have made a commitment—perhaps at confirmation, or more likely, at some time in our adult lives—to follow Jesus, our Lord and our Savior. And on this journey, we are often cold and confused, we struggle with the harshness of winter storms, we try to make our way through the darkness of loneliness or illness or grief.

And on this journey, we need nurturing and we need nourishment. So we turn to God in prayer. We come together in prayer and song, to worship God, to connect with God and with all that is holy. We bring our hearts, hungry to be filled. We bring our tired bodies. We come with heavy burdens. We come with worries. And at the altar, in front of the stable on this Christmas, we can leave our burdens. We can offer our lives—such as they are—to Jesus, knowing that Jesus understands what our life is all about. Jesus lived in the world in which we live.

"It was a chilly night in Bethlehem. People escaped the cold, damp air and crowded into the little inn at the end of the street. They had left their donkeys and camels in the back stable, had shut the door, and were now laughing and chatting with distant relatives they had not seen in years. Family ties were

renewed over bowls of hot soup and goblets of wine. People broke bread together, swapping stories about their long journey. A young boy strummed his lyre, and several fathers clapped their hands in time to the music.

"While balancing a tray of meats and breads, the innkeeper answered a knock at the door. A man calling himself Joseph stood outside, with his cloak pulled tightly around his head. It was late, cold, and he and his young wife who was heavy with child needed a room. The innkeeper could barely hear because of the noise, but he managed to explain that there was no room—only an empty stall or two in the back stable. The innkeeper quickly apologized and slammed the door shut against Joseph.

"Outside, Joseph stood and listened to the laughter behind the door. He sighed deeply, turned, and quietly led Mary to the stable. While a celebration of music and feasting continued inside the warm and bright inn, yards away, the Son of God quietly entered history."[6]

Christmas is a time for children of all ages: a time to smell the holly, the pine trees, the poinsettias, perhaps the chestnuts roasting. Christmas is a time to hear, *really hear* the words of the beautiful Christmas carols. It is a time to wonder at the reflection of the Christmas tree lights, the starlight, the moonlight, glistening across the land, a time to be a child again and trust again and love again.

"But when the fullness of time had come, God sent his Son, born of a woman, born under the law, in order to redeem those who were under the law, so that we might receive adoption as children. And because you are children, God has sent the Spirit of his Son into our hearts, crying, 'Abba! Father!' So you are no longer a slave but a child, and if a child then also an heir, through God" (Galatians 4:4-7).

O Holy Night!
The stars are brightly shining
It is the night of the dear Savior's birth.
Long lay the world in sin and error pining
'Til He appear'd and the soul felt its worth.
A thrill of hope, the weary world rejoices
For yonder breaks a new and glorious morn!
Fall on your knees,
O hear the angels voices.
O night divine,
O night when Christ was born.
O night divine,
O night divine,
O night divine.

O HOLY NIGHT

Bittersweet Night

ilent night? Holy Night? All is calm? All is bright?

Take some time to reflect on what Christmas—that first Christmas—was really like. Consider your own expectations about Christmas, the ideal Christmas and the real Christmas. Mike Royko, the late columnist of the *Chicago Tribune,* wrote about what it might be like if Mary and Joseph were to come to the big city today, for the birth of Jesus. The tale he told described a very confused Mary and Joseph, rejected, disappointed by the "system," basically ignored, and their baby simply a statistic.

Reading the song of Mary, the Magnificat, and the song of Zechariah, the Benedictus, does point to the splendor and the wonder of the Incarnation and the blessings of those close to the Christmas story. But they do not reflect the bittersweet quality of the nativity, which is our own bittersweet heritage today.

Ordinarily, a woman like Mary would have given birth with her mother and other women with her, to comfort her, to ease her anxiety, to help her in the birthing. Instead, Mary and Joseph were alone together at the birth. They were far from home.

The rejoicing and the celebration that were supposed to accompany the birth of a firstborn son were absent—the festivities and the singing and dancing with family and community. Jesus was born in a cold little stable, with only the love of Mary and Joseph to welcome him into the world and keep him warm and unaware of the poverty of it all.

What is the impact of the reality of the nativity, of the bittersweet night when the son of God was born in a stable, far away from home? What is the impact of that bittersweet reality upon you as a busy, contemporary Christian?

We know that the world is not perfect; celebrating Christmas in the reality of our present circumstances may be a challenge. It is true—there is evil in the world, perhaps very close to us. There is poverty, there is hatred, there is mean-spiritedness, none of which take a break just because the calendar says December 25th. This is, we know, the most dangerous time of year for people dealing with depression and alcoholism and chemical dependency. The loneliness and the emptiness in the lives of some of our brothers and sisters in this world may overshadow them. Memories of Christmases past can lead us either to long for the "good old days" or to lament that we never really had a "merry little Christmas."

Now it doesn't make sense to say, "Cheer up! It could be worse!" "Forget your troubles for a day." "Get with it! Some people are REALLY suffering!" No! There is no perfect Christmas. There is rarely a time without illness and death, a time when everyone truly loves one another; a time when all of the masks are taken off and we come together as we really are.

The reality is that we come to Christmastide with our pain and anger and frustration, with our dashed hopes, with our doubts, with our fatigue. We come to a church that it is not a perfect community, perhaps one in which there is tension—right here and right now—and in which there are some members who feel very alienated from the Lord.

Should we give up and sleep away Christmas? No! Let us simply approach Christmas honestly, knowing that the Savior's birth was bittersweet, that his life on earth was filled with conflict and paradoxes. We are invited to come to the feast—just as we are. There are few requirements: simply, that we admit that we need the Lord's grace and blessings and forgiveness, and that we admit that we need to really look for the face of Christ in those we encounter on our Christian journey.

How can we celebrate when everything is not right with the world? Well, to start, we must admit that there is no such thing as pure joy or pure sadness in this life. In *Creative Ministry*, Henri Nouwen wrote, "Celebration can only come about where fear and love, joy and sorrow, tears and smiles can exist together....We can indeed make our sorrows, just as much as our joys, a part of our celebration of life in the deep realization that life and death are not opponents but do, in fact, kiss each other at every moment of our existence."[7]

Perhaps the bittersweet quality of this season will fill us with real understanding, patience, and an infusion of hope, as did the birth of Jesus of Nazareth so many years ago.

Away in a manger, no crib for a bed,
The little Lord Jesus laid down his sweet head.
The stars in the bright sky
looked down where he lay,
The little Lord Jesus asleep on the hay.
Be near me, Lord Jesus! I ask you to stay
Close by me forever and love me, I pray.

AWAY IN A MANGER

Following Jesus

ISAIAH 60:1-6 AND
MATTHEW 2:1-12

t has become a joke among those who study theology that Jesus had many friends, but not one of them was a theologian. What does that say about theologians? Well, I think this is something to consider as we celebrate the feast of the three kings, the Solemnity of Epiphany.

If someone had decided to craft the nativity stories to make a point, surely they would have emphasized that the first ones to hear of the birth of Jesus were the destitute, the shepherds. And later, of course, kings and wise men would have flocked to see Jesus, and they would have brought the finest gifts. But these gifts would have paled in comparison to the humble gifts of Mary and Joseph and the poor folks who surrounded the manger where Jesus was placed after he was born.

Jesus without theologians? I don't think so. But what is theology? And who are the bonafide theologians? *Theology—theo-logos*—is simply "the knowledge of God." Really, all those who seek to know God can be called "theologians." There is nothing in the definition that demands a Ph.D. or an M.Div. In fact, most of us, when asked who taught us the most about God, would probably name an elderly grandparent or aunt or uncle whose connection to God was rock solid.

At the same time, we probably all know persons who are "well-educated" who seem to have no understanding at all of real life or of the important issues that face us every day. Of course, there are people who are well-educated and who also have a deep knowledge of God. This is simply to state the obvious: that there is more to knowing God than book learning.

Was Mary, the mother of Jesus, a theologian? Did she know God? Did she seem to want to be more and more in tune with God? Did she grow throughout her years with Jesus to understand more clearly what God expects from those who profess to love? What about Joseph, about whom we know only that he turned to God and trusted in God and tried to do God's will no matter what the cost? Was he a theologian?

And what about Martha and Mary? Did they know God and ever seek to know God more? And what about Peter and John, who worked as fishermen, but who recognized when to leave that behind to follow Jesus? And what about Paul, who was shaken into service and who followed Jesus in spite of all that he was taught in the Temple?

There are people who ask, "Were there really wise men? Was there really a star? Did people really understand who Jesus was even when he was a baby?" And while we might say these are foolish questions, which only cloud the real issues, I think we ought to clarify for ourselves what is essential to our response to the birth of Jesus, to the coming of Jesus into this world.

In the quiet of these moments, I ask you to consider how you would answer the following questions: How would you welcome Jesus into this world? How would you celebrate the Incarnation of God's only begotten Son into this imperfect world? What would you sacrifice to find him? What dangers would you face? Would you be willing to leave home and family, leave comfort and safety, leave everything behind to follow a star to try to find Jesus?

And what would you bring with you? Would you find something in your home to bring to your Lord and Savior? What precious gift would you bring? Surely, you would spare no expense. Surely, you would bring what is most valuable to you, and you would wrap the gift carefully, and you would go.

Well, then, how far would you go? Would you travel a mile? Would you travel a day? Would you travel to a faraway place where you had never been? Would you spend the rest of your life and all your time and energy to go and meet him, to meet Jesus? And when you arrived, would you recognize the Savior? And would he know you?

Friend, remember this—you have already met Jesus. And you came as you were, and you brought only your humble self and your meager gifts. You have met Jesus and you didn't have to go very far, and you didn't have to sacrifice everything, and you didn't have to walk through the darkness. In fact, Jesus came more than halfway to meet you. He sought you out, picked you out of the crowd of all God's children, and Jesus called you by name, and welcomed you, and invited you to be his servant, saying, "Come, follow me!"

Knowing all this, how do you prepare to encounter Jesus? Further, knowing that you encounter Jesus often, that you meet him in your ordinary day-to-day existence, that you are sometimes surprised by these meetings, that Jesus comes even though you know you are not worthy...how do you meet him? How have you met him? What gifts do you bring? You don't have gold, frankincense, and myrrh. You have only you.

But, wait. What do you see when you look into the creche? Do you see riches and majesty? Do you see royalty as you imagine it to be? No, you see a child in a stable with his mother. Or you see a young prophetic teacher challenging authority in the Temple. Or you see a man rejected for his unpopular views, condemned for teaching the law of love. Or you see the man on the cross, dying in agony for you.

And you know that only one gift is appropriate—all that you are, all that you hope to become, all that God has given to you. This is what you need to give to your King, to Jesus, the Christ. "The wise still seek him." We hear that phrase a lot at this time of year. And it is true that persons who are wise can never be truly satisfied with worldly rewards, with degrees or accolades or honors, or even with earthly knowledge. Even the most intelligent person on earth has nothing without a much more important knowledge, the knowledge of God.

This is a difficult period for some of us, after the Christmas things are put away, and when the depth of the winter becomes real to us. We can become discouraged and sad. It may be helpful to remember that the search for Jesus, which consumed the shepherds, which captivated the wise men from the East, which has ruled the hearts of many through history, continues in us. "Seek the Lord and you will find him." "Seek Jesus and he will find you."

We three kings of Orient are,
Bearing gifts we traverse afar
Field and fountain,
Moor and mountain,
Following yonder star.
O star of wonder, star of night,
Star with royal beauty bright,
Westward leading, still proceeding
Guide us to the perfect Light.

WE THREE KINGS OF ORIENT ARE

Continuing the Watch: Jesus, Simeon, and Anna

LUKE 2:22-40

"My God, Let me just be faithful. Let me just be available, so that you can do your mighty works. We are old friends. We have walked together for as long as I can remember...You have taught me, led me, shown your face to me. Just now let me walk faithfully, By your side, Gently, and in great confidence. Let me watch the creation of your New Jerusalem."[8]

EDWINA GATELEY

 remember very clearly presenting our new-born son to his great-grandmother. I remember how Grandma welcomed our baby into her arms and into the world, how she marveled at the wonder of new life even as she was beginning to walk through the last years of her own life. Dying and living. Death and new life. We see it all around us. We who are older are in awe of the little ones, and yet we know that we are connected to one another. We are all children of the one Creator God.

Angels. Shepherds. Wise men. The gospels tell of many who greeted Jesus shortly after his birth. These accounts testify not only to the wonder of the Incarnation, but also to the fact that Jesus was born into a family *and* into a community. And that community extends to us today. After the birth of Jesus, lives began to change.

Once again, we read the gospel narratives about Anna and Simeon, who were at the Temple when Jesus was brought there a week after he was born to be named in a proper religious ceremony. Whatever their long lives had been about up until that point, the truth is that Anna and Simeon found the true meaning for their lives near the end. When Simeon had his epiphany, he could say to God, "Now I can die in peace, because I have seen your salvation."

In the Temple, at the heart of the life and worship of the Hebrew community, we meet Anna, who had been a widow for longer than many people live. Anna spent her time praying and fasting, dedicating herself to God. Anna was a prophet—she was wise in divine matters, a wisdom probably related to her long life and to her complete devotion to God. Anna's wisdom—a gift from God—enabled her to be receptive to God and to recognize Jesus immediately when Joseph and Mary brought Jesus to the Temple. She praised God for sending the Savior. All those years when she was alone, when she had no real place in society, she had held on because of her faith in God, and then, during her last years, she had her epiphany. Anna was not only a prophet, she was a witness to Jesus; this gave her life meaning.

And so it is for you and me. Our witnessing to Jesus is what really gives meaning to our lives. But Mary...how the birth of Jesus must have changed her! From the moment of that wonderful night when Jesus was born, Mary learned what many of us who are parents know all too well—that our children grow as they separate from us. The presentation of Jesus at the Temple may have been the first time Mary was confronted with the relationship she would have with her son, the powerful reality that Jesus would inevitably grow more separate from her, but that whatever happened to him would still affect her. Whatever he would suffer, she would feel as well. The pain of separation, which all parents feel to some extent, must have been particularly sharp for Mary.

The words of Simeon, "A sword will pierce your own soul, too," rang out painfully against the backdrop of the glorious nativity, and we are all brought back to the truth of that one life—the life of Jesus, stripped of all fanfare, devoid of bright lights and trumpets. For a long time, Jesus was simply attending to the day-after-day stuff of growing up—dealing with the peaks and valleys of life, dealing with the monotony, the sameness, the routine of life, marked by only occasional special events. Most likely, Jesus had a relatively quiet childhood, but nothing is recorded about that time, except for another scene in the Temple, when he was twelve and Mary and Joseph found him after three frantic days of searching. This, too, was an event filled with pain and confusion, as Jesus came to understand more fully his role in the Temple and in the community, and as Mary came to understand that she could not protect her son from life and that she could not protect herself from losing him.

Just as Mary was not spared the pain of separation, we who are on earth to nurture one another—our children, or our sisters and brothers, or others in our community—have no claim upon God's other children. Our relationships are a gift from God, not something we own or possess. Others leave us by growing up, or by going away, or by dying. Every step toward self-actualization, toward independence, toward fulfillment, is marked by separation.

Christmas day has come and gone, but we live in the afterglow of a day that has changed us irrevocably. As we begin to put away our Christmas things, as we take our gifts out of their boxes and put them in with our belongings, we approach the end of the calendar year.

In the last few days of the year, some of us look back at the year that is almost over and try to evaluate our life. Was it better this year than last? What will it be like next year? Some are preparing New Year's resolutions, in order to make the future better. I do it, too. And yet, I wonder if I am putting artificial brackets around my life. Comparing 1999 to 1995 or 1972 is very limiting. It's very subjective, and I tend to forget a lot of smaller blessings while focusing only on larger issues, good or bad. We can only really evaluate at the end of our life—if we have that luxury. So when we try to evaluate a short period of our life and then extrapolate into our entire existence, we usually fall short. We do not yet have the full perspective from which to judge the value of our life.

So how can we satisfy that urge to evaluate, that

need to say, "How am I doing on the journey of life?" Why not concentrate on the things that really matter: Was I more loving this year? Was I more responsive to God in my life? Was I more attentive to my sisters and brothers? Did I devote more of my time to those things that matter—family, church, community—and less time to things that don't—money and power and achievement? Did I make the world a better place by even one act of kindness? Did I ask forgiveness from God and from my neighbor when I faltered? Was I true to my faith, even when that involved taking a risk? Did I stand up for the oppressed—whether my neighbor down the road or my neighbor in some foreign country? Have I learned from my mistakes—not to be perfect, but to be careful and to persevere? Do I look for the face of Christ in others, particularly in those difficult people in my life? Do I see myself as a child of God, and do I care for myself accordingly? Am I willing to keep on keeping on, seeking God until God finds me, serving God until God takes me home?

As this year draws to an end, stay close to the one who came. As your reading of the gospel birth narratives has shown, everyone who encountered Jesus experienced both joy and hardship—John the Baptist, Anna and Simeon, Mary. Ask God's help to deal with the joys and costs of waiting for Jesus, of meeting Jesus, of witnessing to Jesus. Perhaps you can begin with the peace prayer of Saint Francis:

Lord, make me an instrument of your peace.
Where there is hatred, let me sow love.
Where there is injury, pardon.
Where there is doubt, faith.
Where there is darkness, light.
And where there is sadness, joy.
O Divine Master, Grant that I may not
so much seek to be consoled as to console;
to be understood as to understand;
to be loved, as to love.
For it is in giving that we receive,
it is in pardoning that we are pardoned.
And it is in dying that we are born
to eternal life. Amen

PRAYER OF ST. FRANCIS

Joy to the world! The Lord is come:
Let earth receive her King;
Let every heart prepare him room,
And heaven and nature sing.
He rules the world with truth and grace,
And makes the nations prove
The glories of his righteousness
And wonders of his love.

JOY TO THE WORLD

A Happy Renewal Year

ECCLESIASTES 3:1-15 AND
REVELATION 21:1-7

ife is full of contradictory experiences. We hear the story from Scripture:

"For everything there is a season, and a time for every matter under heaven: a time to be born, and a time to die; a time to plant, and a time to pluck up what is planted; a time to keep silence, and a time to speak; a time to love, and a time to hate; a time for war, and a time for peace."

You are a faithful and good person. You trust God and accept whatever happens to you and your loved ones—most of the time. Sometimes, though, you are puzzled by the paradoxes of life—some very good people are suffering, and some very bad people are prospering. From time to time, you look around, and ask, "Why?" and "How?" You pray to the Lord that you would understand life. You know that miracles are everywhere, but sometimes you see only disappointment and pain. You are confused by what you observe.

A Jewish tale advises, "Whenever you see a wicked person who is prospering, keep in mind that his wickedness will ultimately work against him. And if you see a righteous person enduring hardships, remember that perhaps that person is being saved from something worse. Do not doubt these things any longer. One cannot always understand all of God's ways."[9]

Life is uncertain. When we turn the pages of our calendar into a new year, we don't know what is in store. But we are sure of two things: we cannot keep time from passing, and we want this year to be better than last year. Now that we are past the winter solstice, the days are becoming longer. The world is preparing for renewal.

In the hope of improving life, some folks traditionally make New Year's resolutions. Many resolutions are promises to ourselves to change habits or to force new behaviors that don't seem to happen naturally for us yet. How often are resolutions successful? If there is a high failure rate, could it be because we've made decisions about our life without actually thinking about what we need and want, and what is good for us as persons, as children of God, as followers of Jesus? After all, improving our life may be painful. Walking the journey with Jesus means that I own responsibility for my part in what was unsatisfactory behavior. I accept responsibility for my part in what is and what will be new behavior. It is not a matter of punishing ourselves for past mistakes, hating ourselves for past failures, and depressing ourselves with feelings of worthlessness.

Walking the Christian walk involves finishing the unfinished business of my past and choosing to live in new ways that will not repeat old unsatisfactory situations. In the full Christian meaning of the word, "progress" involves repentance and openness to change, and that is a process.

Are you ready to pay attention to God in your life? God says, in the Book of the prophet Jeremiah, "'For surely I know the plans I have for you,' says the LORD, 'plans for your welfare and not for harm, to give you a future with hope. Then when you call upon me and come and pray to me, I will hear you. When you search for me, you will find me; if you seek me with all your heart'" (29:11-13).

Think about what you want for yourself this coming year. Let go of the standard resolutions for a while and look inside for what you really want for yourself. Get in touch with your inner life. Concentrate on your heart. What secret vision for your life do you hold in your heart? What would make you truly happy? Think about this. Imagine it in all its detail. See it. Feel it. Touch it. Hear it.

Move ahead with your life. Hold your vision for the future in your mind and heart. Affirm it now and as often as you can until it becomes real. Do the things you must do to make it happen, and trust that God will support you. Trust that the new heaven and the new earth can begin now in small ways, in sudden moments of wonder, in times of prayer and work. And no matter what the new year brings, you will be whole and safe and strong.

"See, the home of God is among mortals...he will wipe every tear from their eyes. Death will be no more; mourning and crying and pain will be no more....And the one who was seated on the throne said, 'See, I am making all things new.'"

We may be at a crossroads in our life. We do not understand everything that happens—we may be worried about what this year will bring—but we walk with the faith that there is a purpose, a time for every purpose under heaven.

While shepherds watched their flocks by night,
All seated on the ground,
The angel of the Lord came down
And glory shone around.
All glory be to God on high
And on the earth be peace
Good will henceforth from heav'n to all
Begin and never cease.

WHILE SHEPHERDS WATCHED

Summing It Up

LUKE 10:23-24

hen turning to the disciples, Jesus said to them privately, 'Blessed are the eyes that see what you see! For I tell you that many prophets and kings desired to see what you see, but did not see it, and to hear what you hear, but did not hear it.'"

So, how can you celebrate Christmas, in the midst of your busy and complex life as a contemporary Christian? How can you make the most of the story of Jesus coming into our world?

Say "Yes" to What Is!

Acknowledging where we are, what's going on in our lives—the joy and the pain and everything in between—empowers us to celebrate, perhaps quietly, what God has given us. The greatest gifts are ours—the light of the world, the glory of the Lord, God's radiance reflected in our hearts. And, thank God, we have been granted another Christmas season to recall the Incarnation of Jesus Christ— our Lord and Savior—and his continuing companionship with us as we walk our journey through life, on the good days and on the not-so-good days.

Celebrate by Remembering

We all have memories of Christmas—as children, as young adults, as family. And we have to admit that, although the memories may not be perfect, we have been sustained through the many Christmases of our life so that today we are STILL following Jesus, STILL being touched by the love of the season, STILL being moved to imitate the gracious love of God, who sent Jesus to us.

Celebrate by Looking Ahead

Many of us have trouble "staying in the moment"; we're distracted by yesterday's problems and worried about what tomorrow will bring. At Christmastide, we can look forward and be comforted. As we celebrate the Incarnation—that awesome gift from God—we can look forward to a time when the promises that Jesus proclaimed while on this earth will be fulfilled. It's hard to deny that Jesus experienced the full range of human emotions—joy and sorrow, anguish and anger, compassion and pity.

When Jesus died, what seemed to be the ultimate tragedy was turned upside down, because of the Resurrection! We live with the promise that we, too, will rise, that we will live forever in a far, far better state.

Depending on our circumstances, Christmastide can hold incredible joy and incredible pain, often within the same heart. We acknowledge, too, the pain of people who are alone at Christmas, forgotten by kin, ill, exhausted, despairing. We remember and hold in our hearts ALL the children of God.

It came upon the midnight clear,
That glorious song of old,
From angels bending near the earth
To touch their harps of gold:
"Peace on the earth, good will to all,
From heaven's all-gracious King";
The world in solemn stillness lay
To hear the angels sing.
For, lo, the days are hastening on,
By prophet seen of old,
When with the ever-circling years
Shall come the time foretold,
When peace shall over all the earth
Its ancient splendors fling,
And all the world give back the song
Which now the angels sing.

IT CAME UPON THE MIDNIGHT CLEAR

Blessing for Christmastide

Peace to you, Friend, at Christmastide. May you live as Jesus did, taking the world as it is, and bringing to it love and compassion. May you delight in your children and your grandchildren, in your family and friends. May you welcome the stranger, knowing that Jesus came as a stranger into a world that was challenged to recognize him.

May you find the Christ-child wherever you turn. And may your heart be filled with the Joy of Christmas, which is hope; the Spirit of Christmas, which is peace; and the heart of Christmas, which is love!

May God—Creator, Savior, and Holy Spirit—go with you.

Amen

Notes

1. Thurmond, Howard. *The Mood of Christmas*, Richmond, IN: Friends United Press, 1985.
2. Levertov, Denise. *Breathing the Water*, New York, NY: New Directions Publishing Corp., 1987.
3. Johnson, Ann. *Miryam of Nazareth: Woman of Strength and Vision*, Notre Dame, IN: Ave Maria Press, 1984.
4. Anderson, Joan Wester. *Where Angels Walk: True Stories of Heavenly Visitors*, New York, NY: Ballantine, 1992.
5. Young, Carrie. *Nothing to Do But Stay: My Pioneer Mother*, Iowa City, IA: University of Iowa Press, 1991.
6. Tada, Joni Eareckson. *Diamonds in the Dust*, Grand Rapids, MI: Zondervan Publishing House, 1993.
7. Nouwen, Henri. *Creative Ministry*, New York, NY: Doubleday, 1971.
8. Gateley, Edwina. *I Hear a Seed Growing*, Trabuco Canyon, CA: Source Books, 1990.
9. Schram, Peninnah. *Chosen Tale: Stories Told by Jewish Storytellers*, Northvale, NJ: Jason Aronson, Inc., 1997.